Survival Time

poems

Simona Carini

Survival Time © Simona Carini, 2022
Cover Photo © Simona Carini, 2022
Author Photos © Juliana Dean Photography, 2022

ISBN: 9798985524246
Library of Congress Control Number: 2022940873

Sheila-Na-Gig Editions Russell, KY
Hayley Mitchell Haugen, Editor
www.sheilanagigblog.com

In *Survival Time* Simona Carini's poems function as their own microcosms—small wild sanctuaries—where the speaker is free to explore the depths of natural and unnatural dangers. Cancers become scalpels that slice sunlight, but the speaker persists, "Kelp-flavored air / in my lungs, I bloom here too." Though it's not the questioning or the answering that alone make this collection unique, but rather the dance of the polemic itself, *"What does the doctor say?* Brown pelicans / are the coolest birds."

—Kimberly Burwick, author of *Out Beyond the Land*, Carnegie Mellon University Press

The poems in Simona Carini's *Survival Time* are lyrical reverberations of the spiritual relationship between humans and nature. Her poems investigate the complexity of anticipatory grief coupled with fierce hope and unmitigated love. Carini embraces the sensuous immediacy of burning onions, "scarlet bracts," "slit-skin raw landscape" and star-studded damselfish. With profound insight, Carini meditates on the nature of hope—underwater creatures who know the stars, a paper boat sent to sea, or the breath which leaves no trace.

—Nancy K. Pearson, author of *The Whole by Contemplation of a Single Bone*, Fordham University Press

ACKNOWLEDGMENTS

My gratitude to all the people whose comments on the poems have been invaluable. You are all in my heart.   Many thanks to the editors who first published the following poems:

American Journal of Nursing: "Conversation"
California Writers Club Literary Review: "End of Summer in Northern California," "Total Lunar Eclipse"
Intima, A Journal of Narrative Medicine: "Diagnosis," "I Asked My Friend How She Feels: Her Response," "Young Woman Listens to Cyndi Lauper During Dialysis"
Italian Americana: "December 31," "The Fourth of Seven," "Remembering Venice"
Journal of Humanistic Mathematics: "Our Binary World"
Marin Poetry Center Anthology: "*Eremo delle carceri*"
North Coast Journal: "At Butcher Slough," "Dryads Live in Sitka Spruce"
OASIS Journal: "Waiting Area"
Redwood Writers Poetry Anthology: "On the Shoreline," "The Picnic Table," "Solitude," "The Standup Paddler," "We Live on the California North Coast," "Yellowtail Damselfish"
Seven Gill Shark Review: "Erasure"
Sheila-Na-Gig online: "Carson Pass," "The Crypt," "Eternal," "Life on the Edge," "Lærdal Tunnel," "On the Golden Circle, Iceland," "Poppy Blooming," "Rock and Light," "*Rondoni*"
Star 82 Review: "The Bench," "Blue," "Devotion"
Tiny Seed Literary Journal: "Addendum to the *Canticles of the Creatures* Written on the California North Coast," "Driftwood"
Tipton Poetry Journal: "The Body's Refusal to Function as Intended"

CONTENTS

For
Robert

Lærdal Tunnel

Bare rock overhead presses on both sides.
For 20 minutes, deep inside
this Norwegian mountain,
I travel, hold on to the sense
of forward motion.

This is happening to us, not only to me,
you said. I inhaled deeply,
from a place where my fears lodged,
of seeing you in pain—ceasing
to breathe, to relish life with me.

Only the tunnel and no laughing.
We accepted smiles when thanking
white coats for bad news.
Meta, chemo, radio:
full terms truncated, tamed.

At the beginning, familiar words sounded stilted,
How did you sleep? an evasion,
Would you like some fish for dinner? insensitive.
But we still wanted to talk, go for a walk,
not into exile from each other.

Five minutes in, the ceiling rises,
the walls recede, as if the tunnel is breathing in,
and the air turns blue, soft and brilliant:
a deep pool in sunlight. Deeper
into the mountain, dark again.

When you have cancer, your life
is called survival time. Time scale changes
from years to months. Birthdays,
anniversaries erased from the calendar.
Instead, blood tests, scans, visits, drug refills.

The tunnel expands into a blue hall again,
yellow light peeks from the floor, hinting at sunrise.
Azure washes my face, like diving
into the Caribbean Sea looking for my favorite
damselfish: blue with stars on its body.

We've learned to discuss your bike rides,
my writing, the ocean, details that define us—
not birthdays or anniversaries, but the days at home
dancing around the stove, car trips with the cats, nights
in our bed, staring in silence at the new moon.

To My Breath

One day I'll let you go, will have no choice,
won't see you leave, won't know you've left. No more
scent of jasmine, sweet peas, the sea. No more
panting as I run among the trees and you
float as clouds in daybreak's cold. I trust
I'll smile when I last breathe, but now I fear
the day you will no longer come and go.
Will my final sigh be the last sound I hear?
Will I recall the seal to my one life?
I practice Shavasana—the yoga
corpse pose—slacken muscles and joints, exhale,
pause, listen to silence within. Without
your constant flow, a meadow with no breeze,
I want it unperturbed but cannot see it so.

The Fourth of Seven

To get to it crack a cage or thread through a pulsed flow.
Centrally located and four-chambered, it runs with timed
precision, traffic strictly one-way. Works well under pressure,
but a touch, song, gaze, aroma can make it jump or miss a step.

Can be stopped, restarted, jolted back to dance to the right
rhythm, replaced with a gently used one. Valves can be cleaned
of vegetation or changed, electrical system overruled, irrigation
patched. May fail, and there have been cases when breakage

was surmised, but proof remains elusive. It freezes, melts,
yet doesn't change physical state. Tune into its tempo,
hark its pleas—a missed beat, a sudden thump
ricocheting in the throat—breathe into it to open it.

The heart chakra is green.

Conversation

How is he doing? I row at dawn when silence
rules the bay, the marina sleeps, night
thaws into downy dawn, fog hovers on shore, light
diffuses like stereophonic sound from dual speakers.
Above, clear sky, sharp-edged,
unquestionable in its blue righteousness.

What does the doctor say? Brown pelicans
are the coolest birds. They show off, I swear,
fly fast a few inches off the water, aerodynamic,
touch down then drift.
Shooting stars, they dive,
surface, bill full.
Egrets are different.
Still—they scan the water, strike, suck.
A glint quivers and dies,
as if nothing happened.

How are you holding on? Only the oars
to hold on to once I push off the dock.
They keep me balanced as I glide,
the future behind me.
A tide can't always be high,
it ebbs, rolls back.

I row for an hour,
then work, the house, the cats,
take refuge in a no wake zone.
Words go too fast.
Forgive my stillness.

Eremo delle carceri
Hermitage of St. Francis on Mount Subasio, Assisi

The small saint made himself smaller through a narrow space
to enter. On one side he lay down after chanting compline,
the night prayer, slept on bare rock with a stone pillow.
His faith as solid as the cave's walls.

There was a small chapel, but mostly just holm oaks
under whose evergreen shade he paced, prayed, preached.
When I, a petite girl, walked along the *Eremo*'s paths,
St. Francis spoke to me in the voice of leafy branches
rustling, of birds flittering. He touched me in the light
raining from the stately trees.

No longer a girl and far away now, severed from ancient places
where psalms echo, where St. Francis left footprints, kind words
to a wolf, humans, flocks of birds, when I need to see my life's
bedrock I walk into a forest's shade, shut my eyes, enter his cave.

Dryads Live in Sitka Spruce

Not shy as tree nymphs are said to be
not oak-dwelling, but Sitka spruce,
never worry about leaves leaving and
not returning, like dawn-swept dreams.
With Artemis, we see unseen hands
hired to wrench *Dudleya* plants off their native
North Coast. Bluff lettuce, pale green
rosettes of fleshy leaves vermilion-tipped,
erects a stem and blooms with a cluster
of yellow flowers. Not abalone iridescent,
yet coveted, like a nymph by Pan.
Ancient wardens, we whisper suspicion
into ears ready to follow the trail of dirt.
Replanting like healing.
Don't believe in our existence, in dryads
or archer Artemis roaming forests and hills?
Believe the plunder. Tiny *Dudleyas*,
redwood burls, poachers grab: it's what they do.
Spring: our home trees grow fingers of
bright needle-like leaves. We have been here eons.
Artemis too, watchful, unleaving.

Waiting Area

Ten hours waiting for him.
One by one, the names on the glaring monitor disappear.
His name remains "In Surgery."

One by one, relatives, personnel leave.
The last one leaves a light on for me. Do I need anything?
I want "Surgery" to segue into "Recovery" —now.

Is the surgeon chasing cancer cells, struggling
with sutures? I taste acid, like reflux.
The screen does not refresh.

In the cavernous ward
ears strain listening for the surgeon's steps
ticking a countdown to compose myself.

The monitor flickers: "Surgery" surrenders to "Recovery."
The steps stop, I look into exhausted eyes:
… *doing well… on the 9th floor…*

The elevator rises slowly. We meet, clutch hands.
He grins *Ciao* —a word he won't remember saying.
Tomorrow morning, he will ask whether I was there.

Rock and Light

I run among trees, the Pacific
rumbling behind morning
fog, the trail strewn with leaves
and small branches washed
down by storms, past vacant
campsites, picnic tables coated
with moss, empty benches—
no one watching the waves—
a towering rock, sparkling igneous
diamonds. Time deposits
layers on it, erodes them. The park
is mine: greens, browns,
and grays at the horizon. Refined by
quick breathing, I emerge mother
of pearl. As I turn, the sunlight
lancing through Sitka spruce
forms a fan of rays. As a child
I thought it was God.
I still do.

The Picnic Table

We leave the doctor's office in silence, spent as empty saline bags.
We entered in early afternoon, it is evening now. Is it the same day
or a different life?

In the car, my eyelids drop, shutters rolling down at the end
of store hours. My mind a tabula rasa,
except for the certainty of love.

I was running in the park. Leaf litter, mud, puddles. Legacy
from a storm just passed. Fog condensed into stars stuck
to my jacket, clung to my swinging body.

At each inhalation I drank the scent of newborn grass.
A picnic table, upholstered with moss. How many rainstorms
has it weathered? Forest, I prayed, heal him now.

We arrive. I hoist my heavy heart and open the garage door.
Wind, uncloud his sky.

The Crypt

Shady, the Basilica, cool,
light filtering through paned
windows draws a path,
through redwoods it marbles
the ground, a creek or a bird's whisper.
Christ looks down from the apse.
I descend into the crypt,
Saint Ambrose lies in a glass casket—
a skeleton—in bishopric robes.
I sit with him, my holdfast,
with a fallen redwood too,
look for conversation
in places born sacred.

In the Church of St. Christina, Bolsena

Two small footprints
indent a flat basalt stone
dark like a cave,
round like the lake nearby.
Of the child Christina, they say,
tied to it and tossed
into the cobalt blue water
by her father to drown her faith.

Do you believe the story?
A whisper in the still air.

I believe the stone,
see the girl's courage to stand up.
The water beckoned and scared,
she trusted her God
the stone to carry her,
floating cushion,
lay her back on land.
She left her footprints for us to consider.

It wasn't just the stone:
writhing snakes, raging fire,
boiling oil and more:
do you believe all that?

I knew Christina in a dear friend;
most of her life a rock hung around her neck,
a disease intent on drowning her.
She endured storms:
burning rash, joint pain, renal failure—
survived, another struck.
The Passion must end in a place
where pain has no space.
In heaven at peace, agony-free,
she leaves footprints, perfumed petals.

These depressions set in stone
keep the story alive.
I trace them, say goodbye to my friend.
Behind the oxygen mask, with her final sigh,
she dropped her disease, traded it for light.

Addendum to the *Canticle of the Creatures* Written on the California North Coast

From a blue so deep the sky
burns in envy, to a gentle gray a shade
darker than the compact clouds above,
every few hours you don a different
dress, striped or solid, white-
laced or embroidered by emerging
sea stacks.

Rolling in *pianissimo* or raging
to shore, you are best as mirror
to my internal churn. I write edgy
footprints at your door, the tide takes them.
You are worst when your hypnotic
motion lures—waves crawl ashore,
slide back, encore—
then slaps me with cold water.

If fog shrouds you, your roar
lets me know you are there.
Unless I hear you,
how can I be sure of anything?

Praised be You, Brother Ocean:
you fill me. No other so close,
so close to me.

On the Shoreline

Morning walk where water and land meet,
a contour shifted, rewritten by tides.

The ocean lays out presents on the beach: crab's
claws, driftwood, strands of seaweed — a scalpel

at work, I want to wield. I marvel, deposit
dense lines in my mind, still. I catch

a glint of warm amber in cool light,
gather an agate, finger it, a rosary bead.

Formed in volcanic rock, currents
and waves weathered it out of its host,

carved curves, surfaced patterns. A breaker
deposited it on the sand then retreated offshore.

A surfeit of words on my page to plane
down — I summon a force, oceanic.

Yellowtail Damselfish

(Microspathodon chrysurus)

What does an underwater creature know about
the night sky,
the stars in it?

Intense blue studded with diamonds,
a small fish flashes,
sliver of night sky cut from the galaxy's heart.

Juvenile Yellowtail Damselfish
half the size
of its name on the page.

A chance mutation chose night blue,
the next one aimed for the stars.
An easy catch for predators,

until one reduced its stars to dots
as it grew up—and reproduced.
A yellow tail for defense.

Beauty had to become transient.
A malevolent law, cosmic balance—
leave God out of this. Nature handles her own.

Young Jewel Damsel
patrols its coral territory with the fervor
of a newborn star.

Tiny fish in improbable regalia blazes
through muted surroundings
tangoing with my eyes.

Green eyes, ten deft fingers, four-chambered heart,
double circulation I have, yet not that blue,
those stars.

One Hope Ends at the Threshold of the Next

Six weeks after prostatectomy the blood level of PSA should be 0

For forty days we think of nil so hard
it grows a face, a smile. We swallow faith
in daily drams. At night, alone, words fail,
at each deep breath, fear tears with no regard.
The verdict comes online, a number starred
and high: it leaves no ease except in grace.
It stops our pulse. Our hearts, as close in space
as ribs allow, stand still, restart all jarred.
Time skids towards horizon's fatal lure.
My voice is onions burning on the stove.
You touch my back: a bell tolling. We flood,
find ground again: the place where we endure,
where each three weeks a chemo hope dissolved
in saline finds its way into your blood.

At Butcher Slough

Arcata Marsh & Wildlife Sanctuary

No ducks ply the slough,
no great egrets glide. Wrung out
clouds pattern the marsh
in light ink. Air as crisp as
cave-cooled watermelon.

Silence ambushes me
in this quiet place of
still water, wood pilings—
remains of a mill—
an old railway track.

If my worries could ride away!

My lungs catch a scent
I am an egret sensing
fish just beneath the
surface. I dive. Find
gratitude.

A sheet of paper laid on the marsh
absorbs. A *suminagashi** print:
Sky marbled with frayed clouds.
I hang the print to dry, leave it
for others. A gift of thanks.

* the ancient Japanese technique of floating ink (*sumi*) on the surface of water to
create marble-like patterns, which are then transferred to paper dropped on top.

Driftwood

We travel long distances
after we die. Alive,
we grew roots in the place

where our seeds sprouted.
When still green-maned,
we inhaled carbon dioxide,

exhaled oxygen for breathing
beings. After, we shed
our photosynthetic garb,

travel with just trunk,
branches and main roots,
board a current, a tide.

After a life vertical, we discover
horizontal; after holding onto soil
and holding it in place,

we turn into wanderers,
embrace cobalt, teal,
the moon. Waves sculpt us,

the sun bleaches us.
Water-borne, we raft
birds, fish, aquatic species.

Oceanic forces carry us—
storm-dependent, tide-reliant
voyagers—deposit us ashore.

We shelter salamanders,
snowy plovers and other
nesters, trap silt and seeds,

help sea rocket, sand verbena,
dune tansy take root,
tend life where we lie.

We Live on the California North Coast

Blue still catches me by surprise.
Silken sky, ragged ocean meeting
at the horizon—a liquid blue line,
like sealing a pact.

Standing at the continent's edge, I drink
the blue above and below, depend on it
like a beached sea star relies on high tide.

The ocean's breaking into the night.
The sky listens. The two fuse.
You and I float in our embrace—
hawk's wings and whale's flukes.

Remembering Venice

Xe bela, Venessia,
soft voices in the local singsong dialect.
In the canals, the water is clearer:

does it still reflect lights on its inky surface at night?
Locked down like the rest of Italy,
the city is quiet. No one walks along *calli,* across its *campi.*

Are chandeliers alight in the palaces' frescoed rooms?
Under St. Mark Square's deserted arcade, rare steps resound
like castanets, Murano glassware lie in shadow in shuttered stores.

Waves lap against the *fondamente.* No *gondolieri* call out *Òe!*
at canal crossings. No friends sit outside the *bacari* in the quiet
hour laughing loudly over glasses of spritz.

I will visit Venice again, arrive at sunset, fuchsia and dark
orange lighting the city, floating on a lilac mirror—
the water calm as an Alpine lake at dawn.

I will inhale the lagoon's briny scent, bathe
in the radiance of rosy light reflected on windows,
dusk slowly clothing *La Serenissima* in silence.

Emotion will be fierce, like on my last day there, a bright
October Sunday: I walked from first light
until sunset wrapped the city in pink lace.

I walked at night, listened to water, church bells, whispers.
Memories guide me through darkness to morning light
reflected on *Punta della Dogana*'s golden sphere, flashing.

Three Poems
Torres del Paine National Park, Chile, March 2020

Mirador Las Torres

The plane lands: Patagonia—Andean peaks
I dreamed one day of ascending.
The road from Punta Arenas crosses a wind-whipped plain, no blue,
only brown bush under leaden clouds,
a slit-skin raw landscape, my eyes sheer
away from the grim ground strewn with rocks.

At the park's entrance, no bush, just rocks,
in the distance the massif's peaks.
The curtains in the lodge's room, lacy and sheer,
let the outside in. My gaze ascends,
as a breeze chases away the clouds:
backlit by the setting sun, pinnacles haloed by blue.

The morning after, sunrise lights the east pale blue,
sets the granite walls ablaze, massive rocks
emerging from a bank of soft clouds:
Torres del Paine— three towering peaks.
The flashing mountains call me to ascend:
the flank they offer impregnable, sheer.

I cross a valley, enter the sheer
cool nave of a beech forest—the air darkens to blue
among the breeze-swayed gnarled trees, solemn as monks whose
    chant ascends
from choir stalls. Past the woods, the moraine awaits, rocks
piled on steep terrain. I often can't see the peaks:
climb, clasp branches to brace my pilgrimage to the clouds.

Andean condors soar, float weightless: clouds.
High wind, panting, boots crunching gravel, sheer
fatigue focuses me on steady steps towards the peaks.
I hope the sky will turn, for a moment, blue.
The trail levels out: behind a last line of rocks
the vista opens onto the prize for my ascent.

Silence attends the arrival from the hours-long ascension:
the three Torres rise into torn clouds:
prongs of a trident, giant rocks
of gray granite, their sheer
faces unyielding. At their feet, a serene lake of unique blue,
liquid turquoise. A breeze clears the sky around the peaks.

Quickly it is over: a train of clouds wraps around the peaks.
The earlier vision—erased—becomes a rock-solid memory of
    granite and blue.
I descend with it, a sacred relic wrapped in silken sheer.

The Burned Forest

Ashen trunks, bare branches loom
above an expanse of shrubs and saplings
that green the graveyard of the ancient forest,
killed by a man-lit fire.

The trail skirts Lake Skottsberg—a sheet
of silver under the overcast sky—a mirror
for the *Cuernos del Paine*, godlike peaks
of pale granite, topped with dark sediment.

A rumble rolls down the rocky flank:
ice shifting, out of sight. I hike past trees
standing as their own tombs, imagine them
before, dressed in dark green foliage.

I once walked with my father
along the pebbled paths of his village's cemetery
lined with cypresses. Crosses, marble slabs—
photos revealing the faces alive.

Between the mountains and the water
the wooden skeletons and scars.
A single person inflicted this injury.
And flames froze them as though in prayer.

Coming Up for Air

Grey Lake, true to its name, powdery gray,
and dark green hills beneath a pewter sky.

The lone boat steeped in silence draws near
Grey Glacier, light blue—a fairy's tulle gown—

each crevasse a canyon in glowing ice.
Three-lobed, alive, it slowly slides, calves

icebergs into the lake, floating carvings,
paper boats a child sends off on a pond.

On deck, whispers, as in a saint's shrine.
I pray but still a plague deluges the world,

sinks lungs in fluid, pushes lives below
water. A year on, lake and glacier shape

a dream, blue queendom of ice, where I breathe
brisk air and feel my pulse speed up again.

Fractured Phalanx of the Left Fifth Finger

A stream of human frailties flows outside my room:
A man fell from his wheelchair, bruised his face,
a senior's heart beat out of rhythm like a clumsy dancer,
a woman felt weak while walking: low blood glucose,
or loneliness.

The surgeon arrives, a whirlwind of sky-blue scrubs.
He smiles, touches my hand — I'm in no pain — tells me
he'll pin the broken bone.

As if by the tap of a wand, the room fills with nurses
to ready me for surgery. I fall into an inky sleep,
until my eyes open onto a large clock, a later time, a left hand
I explore by touch: padded splint around the little
and ring fingers, elastic bandage from fingertips to wrist,
three fingers free to wiggle like tentacles of a sea star —
self-image cracked like the small bone, a new *manus* to learn
to use for a month of awkward touch.

At home, I cannot hold an onion steady under the sharp blade,
the splint on its own presses the Caps Lock key while I type,
and suddenly my words scream on the screen.
If I close my eyes, I fall again, and the outcome is the same:
a fragile bone snaps on impact. Inside the splint,
I imagine the two bone ends making peace, one again.
But like in my mended bone china cup,
the seam will be visible every time I drink tea.

Carson Pass

On the trail, slanted sun rays
marble rocks with shadows, night's
coolness inhabits the alpine forest.
Snow covers the ground in patches
melting into rivulets.

A dead Sierra juniper stretches out sun-washed,
twisted branches. It will fall and fall apart into
soil supporting seedlings and flowers.
In the company of a dead tree, my fear of dying
dwindles to a small knot loosened by a deep
breath of pine resin-perfumed air.

The trail ahead is lined with wildflowers:
red Indian paintbrush, purple lupine, white
phlox, yellow mule's ears. Above, the bold
blue of a clear summer sky—absolute,
like love.

I jump over running water, hear a rustling nearby:
a cinnamon-colored black bear waddles away.
The moment leaves before I am fully
aware of it. It will be a sweet
aftertaste—of sharp air, sunlight scattering
and a bear's breakfast interrupted.

When a snow patch extends beyond my line
of sight, I turn around. Frog Lake appears,
sapphire ruffled by a breeze.
On the shore, I unpack worries about work,
deadlines, a mammogram's date coming due.
I kneel down, drop them and let them float
away.

Life on the Edge

On the windblown bluff
splashed by salt spray
a tuft of Indian paintbrush—flames
of scarlet bracts—turned
the hostile slope into host.
Kelp-flavored air
in my lungs, I bloom here too.

I Ask My Friend How She Feels: Her Response

On chemo, I open my eyes
and it is always infusion day,
the weeks in between fused.

On chemo, I steep milky tea,
keep constant watch,
as fear stages a coup every hour.

I wash lettuce leaf by leaf
and, short of breath, I smell
cells killed by the drugs, metallic.

On chemo, I drop a frame,
pick up the shards, cannot compose
the full picture.

On chemo, I look around for
my running shoes, the favorite blue shirt I lost,
to put them on again.

On chemo, I watch a blue jay hop,
a squirrel dart and I want off:
off chemicals, off cancer.

I dance a few steps,
an oil-slicked bird thrashing its wings around,
calling it flying.

Poppy Blooming

Sunlight draws a scalpel
along the bud's seam exposing red
flesh. Crumpled petals widen the split
unfolding, unstoppable.

Pale sepals cling to
the past pushed away.
Finally fall—severance.

Red petals stretch,
iron their creases.
Stigma blinks in the sun,
stamens sway in the breeze.

The poppy cannot unbloom, fold
back, shut the bud. I cannot unwrite—
words unfold in their own private sun.

Total Lunar Eclipse

When risen, the full moon is not blood red,
as advertised, but damask rose and blurred
in the dusk sky polluted by streetlamps
and headlights. Sad, I drive back home. At night,
a blade of light across our front yard
signals Selene has changed back to white
attire and whole round shape. I step outside
and hope to see the moon above the trees.
The spruce though, tall and thick, occlude the view.
My eyes are set to shut their lids. I turn
around to go inside. I stop breathing:
the Big Dipper has landed on our roof,
its seven stars button the inky sky,
outline a ladle tilted just enough
to shower stardust on our house.

End of Summer in Northern California

To those
who say our state
has no real fall: Notice
how warmer light paints cliffs ocher
after noon. Walk on roads where pink naked
ladies bloom. Run in Redwood Park and watch deer hop
among ferns turned brown. Hike Sierra trails strewn with golden
leaves showered by quaking aspen. At dawn, crack the frozen
stream near your tent. Fog no longer rolls in at day's
end, chilling you. See the horizon at
sunrise draw a sharp line between
ocean and sky. Hear trees
exhale in our
first rain.

The Body's Refusal to Function as Intended

I take a bite from an apple, make a hollow,
chew slowly, halt: cannot swallow.

When muscles work in concert, in sequence, actions follow.
Not now, though: nothing moves and I cannot swallow.

With effort I shove the bolus down, stow the apple.
Inhaling hurts: I'm lacerated inside by the hard swallow.

I reel and through closed eyes I probe the sorrow:
What is it my body refuses to swallow?

Friends want my help when lovers leave them hollow,
teachers press me towards a choice they want me to swallow.

My parents' grieving silence grinds me: I should live at home
until I marry, work close by—customs I refuse to swallow.

If I cannot feed myself, I'll waste away, turn hollow.
Enough demands and complaints. I'll fly away as my own swallow.

Rondoni

The shrill scream of common swifts at sunset
promised spring: longer days, warmer weather—
summer soon. From the balcony you watched them
dive, whirl, soar, circle—dark slender body,
forked tail, long swept-back wings like crescents,
their flight fast, effortless, their loops, spells.
They would be loud again as summer waned,
a call to prepare to migrate south of the equator.

You yearned to join the swoop, fly to tropical peace, away
from the frigid draft between your parents, your mother's
anger storms, your father's bitter counters. You wanted
to grow wings, rise high, sweep down. One day you left—
by rail. Blizzards never ended at home: you learned
it was not your burden to turn its winter into spring.

In Your Aunt's House in the Village

memories storm your mind, ocean waves against rocks,
you recall the last time you visited, the last time
you stepped inside from the glare of a baking August noon,
the last time she chirped *Eccomi* when you called.
In the penumbra of shuttered windows, past the antique
hard-backed armchair not shrouded in a sheet,
you walk into her bedroom, run your fingers
on her treadle sewing machine, cast-iron on walnut wood cabinet,
she pushed the pedal and the needle moved up and down
up and down, fast, and with fabric you'd chosen from her stash
she sewed the shirt, skirt, or dress you'd drawn on tracing paper.
The umber *credenza* holds bone china demitasse cups and saucers
and the same scent of sugar and anise you savored as a child,
when you opened its creaking glass door looking for candies,
woodworms attacked the table and chairs, but that sweet aroma
has withstood decades, like a bee cast in amber.
Bunches of grapes hung to dry, tall jars of rainbow pickles,
vibrant voices and bouncy steps haunt the rooms
full of familiar objects no longer touched by familiar hands.
You don't owe anything to this house, yet it offers coolness
within its thick stone walls and the old kitchen
to fry fresh eggs, wash lettuce, slice tomatoes,
set a feast on the table.

Telegrams

When a telegram arrived for my *Nonna*,
the house sank into silence broken by soft sobs.
In those days, in rural Italy, telegrams brought
the bad news of someone dead or dying.
Nonno sat still at the table. A boy then, my father asked
his mother: *Why don't you open it?*

She considered her three sons away from home, in Rome—
Domenico, Luciano, Angelino—her cousins, distant relatives,
while the folded paper waited to speak.
After the first tide of tears ebbed, she broke the seal:
'Happy birthday STOP Domenico'

From afar, the eldest son must have smiled
picturing the surprise on his mother's face—
her hand held up to cover her mouth opened into an *O!*
He did not see her tears, nor hear *Nonno*'s swearing.

Smartphone messages do not arrive folded:
three times in the last three months
the screen snared my eyes. There was no
unreading the words. *Ci ha lasciato*—died.

This morning, sunlight filtered through
the redwoods marbling the road. As I warmed up,
the phone chimed, the screen flashed.
I left it in my pocket and began my run.

Eternal

As a child I read tombstones:
Two dates bracket unknown lives.

Who were they
before death fixed their age?

"Eternal" stenciled on the west wall
of a falling-down Berkeley house.

No dates but broken windows
blinded by rotting boards, creeping ivy.

Doors no longer open to welcome,
or closed to secure.

Eternal is not what we build,
the wind breaks the glass.

Who wrote "eternal" on this house?
The owner who hoped.

Exegi monumentum aere perennius
Horace's monument

more lasting than bronze,
words we still recite and

revere after two thousand years.
A brushstroke of brown paint

erases "eternal" from the wall
but the word remains.

Solitude

Our life no longer
a *duet:* a *silo,*
rather, *toils due* to the
god of Fate Chosen.
My *soul tied* to this table
across from you, set in
solid silence. Sing!
My *loudest I* wants
her voice heard. You
duel it so you can
erase the lines
that *lied to us.* What
comes *due I lost.*
My shadow lives in
an *old suite* of stone.
Take these words to
dilute so you can undo
the *old tie* once
gentle between *us.*
Leave me the residue:
solitude

Young Woman Listens to Cyndi Lauper During Dialysis

I want to be the one to walk in the sun-
light, the extra weight I carry shed.

I must shed the extra weight I carry.
They told me fasting made my kidneys fail.

I failed my fasting by eating two lettuce leaves,
had to flush them out or I will never be thin.

I had to flush out the lettuce leaves, thin,
yet they become pounds of fat on my body.

Ninety-five pounds for a five-two body.
Blood is flowing out of my veins, a red rivulet.

I stare at the blood flowing out of my veins
into a whirring machine, then coursing back.

Out of my veins into a machine, back inside me
for hours, I cannot be the one to walk in the sun.

The Bench

Each dot a person life-vest orange.
The luckier ones
packed tightly in a boat
floating rudderless
somewhere in the Mediterranean Sea.
They carry their life:
clothes, papers,
a spoonful of dirt from home
wrapped and held to heart.
The memory of parting,
tearing pages from a book,
worn down and walking
towards a mirage,
a beach, a boat, an empty bench.

Devotion

A strip of mulched soil skirts
the wide cement path.
A power wheelchair is parked
on the side: Empty, and no one's
on the bench nearby.
A rustling of leaves and woodchips
directs my gaze: an old man, thin,
in baggy corduroy pants, plaid shirt
and blue baseball cap kneels on the dirt,
head bowed low, propped on his left hand,
right hand busy weeding
around a plant, his knobby fingers
still nimble at the task.
A worshipper, a flower.

Diagnosis

Feet strapped to my scull, I launch and free
the clock, stall the time drain, my churn, your pain.
Through morning fog the pastel sunrise streams:
Catch, drive, recovery, then catch again.
Slow strokes on water barely awake,
I glide backward towards a future day
I glimpse without your eyes, and leave a wake,
a line, to tell the birds hope's flown away.
My oar blades break the water's silky plane,
their rhythmic dip the loudest sound around,
a measured pulse that drives away the ache,
repels the dark that drags me deep to drown.
I balance on the water seeking grace
to breathe and draw a trace that leaves no trace.

The Standup Paddler

Sunlight streams through coastal Sitka spruce, a thin fog
lingering over the glassy lagoon. A shape glides through the mist:
a stocky, dark-bearded man in black shorty wetsuit
and straw lifeguard hat dips the paddle, pulls it, repeats—
measured moves of a scepter or bishop's crozier. Sphinx-like
on the front of the board, a black and white border collie, eyes
trained on the horizon. A great egret and great blue heron squawk,
fighting for a prized fishing spot. Beyond the sand spit,
the ocean rumbles, out of sight. The pair advances,
parting the sparkling surface. The man nods, paddles on.
Distant, his board invisible, his feet at water level, floating.

Blue

Inside the blue universe,
blue sky, and inside it
blue ocean, and in it
a Juvenile Yellowtail Damselfish,
intense blue studded with diamonds,
heart of the blue nesting doll.

I surfaced slowly from the deep
blue alongside an endangered
turtle, her fore flippers beating
like eagle wings.

I carried the blue home,
sowed cornflower seeds as I walked,
so the way to our house will bloom
blue, a river in reverse—autocorrects
to reverie: blue ocean and a piece
of night sky in the shape
of a small fish.

Erasure

Two sculls slide into
the dwindling water
of a minus tide. We row
as the early sun
peeks over close coastal fog
capping inland hills.
Humboldt Bay. Four oars'
rhythmic dips nick the silence.

Boats bleed into ghosts,
trees fade to traces.
At the south end of
Woodley Island Marina:
fog. No land is visible,
how ancient sailors
imagined the Unknown,
past the Pillars of Hercules.

A familiar place
now a landscape of losses,
like a life bereft. I hold the oars,
the hose, the bucket. A harbor seal,
round head and eyes, surfaces
near the dock. Our gazes lock:
It's just us, dear friend, just us.

Bicycling Around Lake Llanquihue, Chile

The road ahead wraps around the lake,
a scarf of asphalt. Blue water eclipsed,
reappears. Osorno Volcano's glacier-cloaked
peak confirms my route is right.
Beneath its watch I'll reach my goal.
Signs lead to farms with food for sale,
their gardens riots of giant-headed dahlias,
fireworks in glaring sunlight.
My feet push pedals towards 100 kilometers—
a rhythm, like breathing. I defy headwind,
rough road, stop for water at Las Cascadas.
The guide offers me a bowl of blueberries:
arándanos. Avid teeth crush pearls of juice,
purple-blue lips smile. Kindness tastes sweet,
lifts me up one more hill, my finish line.

On the Golden Circle, Iceland

Geyser Strokkur hurls water at the sky:
the spout collapses, sprays around. A pause,
again: Hot water explodes at each beat
of earth's boiling heart. Up the road, Gullfoss:
the Hvítá river falls then falls again.
We stand a step away from cancer's lurch:
the reins will fail and death approach and pound
like water the rock floor. Until that day,
I need no geyser nor cascade, but crave
lava fields softened by ancient moss
that grows at coral's speed, Icelandic horse
and I trotting on Viking trails all breeze
and drizzle. I smell wet earth, horse's sweat,
taste nostalgia for a place not yet left
and ache for someone not yet lost.

December 31

Some days there is no horizon, no
edge where the Pacific dips and the sky rises.
Blue—your eyes, the evening air—a flock
of shorebirds running behind a retreating
wave, raking the wet sand with quick beaks,
then backing away from the wave washing
ashore. Again, and again, like breathing. The end
arrives with our last breath. A long sigh the last
sound we make. We carry nothing with us,
not even a gulp of air. Will I, on the final
exhale, remember kindness in your gaze?
The shorebirds never rail against the coming
wave for being early, too strong: they accept
the aftermath, the food the ebbing water leaves.
Drenched in the last light of the year, just wait,
you are not alone.

Our Binary World

I learned to count as incantation,
grasping unity with one hand, duality
with the other, bringing them together into
one universe, two trillion galaxies, one body,
37.2 trillion cells (double that, if counting resident microbes),
individual, dual and myriads.

I learned to count in binary to touch again
the magic, an effort not to lose count, not to miss
the trail of crumbs that is life:
0
1
10
11
100
101
110
111
1000
1001
1010, decimal 10 duplicated—incantation again.

Only 0 and 1, dual—not "us versus them"
rather, the complement of you and I among myriads.

By 1 and 0 we cover the distance between the dream
of the other and the tie that binds us at the heart.
1, I say, 0, you respond, and we laugh until resonance
shatters memories of couples past, undams love.

0, can you pick up the mail? 1, can you take out the garbage?
Of 0's and 1's is our life together made, of small tasks
and hours with or without them. The stream pushes onward
to meet the ocean.

Simona Carini was born in Perugia, Italy. She writes poetry and nonfiction and has been published in various venues, in print and online. She lives in Northern California with her husband, loves to spend time outdoors, and works as an academic researcher. Her website is https://simonacarini.com